CONVERSATIONS

Stories and Poems
That Speak to Our Soul

williamrbs@aol.com

William R. Stephenson, PhD

outskirts
press

TABLE OF CONTENTS

Chapter Three - Recovery with Others

Chapter Four - The Season of Beginnings and Beginnings Again

ACKNOWLEDGEMENT

This is my third book of poetry and story related to my work with persons struggling with a life-threatening illness, those who had suffered a significant loss of a loved one or witnessed a particularly emotional event. Putting these cases into poetry or story was my way of affirming the work and courage of my clients. I want to acknowledge, first of all, these wonderful clients, many of them children, adolescence and young adults who would permit me to be a part of their lives for such a short time. I also want to thank their families and friends who gave so much support to these clients.

To the congregation called Water's Edge, an alternative worshiping community of the First United Methodist Church of San Diego. They were often the "first receivers" of a story or poem. They listened, gave feedback and encouraged me to listen to my soul.

As I did with my second book, so also with this one, all of the proceeds realized in the sale of this book will be donated to support the ministries of Water's Edge, such as Rachel House for abused women.

CHAPTER ONE
THE POWER OF LOVE

JERSEY BOY

His name was Anthony. He was nine years old and from Jersey Shores. He was a kid who loved the beach and sand so much he practically lived there. But he had cancer.

Bone cancer. Initially in the spine, and it was spreading rapid-
ly. He came out to California to participate in an experimental
trial, but his chances were not good. I was asked to be part of
his care as counselor to him and his family.

Anthony liked to draw. That was going to be my way of
getting through to him. We started to draw together, almost
competitively. But the rule I expected us to both follow was
to describe or explain what the drawing meant, or how we
felt about what we had drawn. We spent many hours drawing
and talking with each other about our drawings and about
our lives.

"Dr. Bill, what are you drawing today?"

"I'm drawing the house I grew up in. Would you like to
see it?"

"Why did you draw this house today and not yesterday?"

"Anthony, your intuition is incredible. Because today is
the day my father died and I was home at the time I was
told of his death. I drew the house today to remember him.
Anthony, what would you draw that will help others remem-
ber you?"

He thought about this for several moments, and then he
said, "I would draw myself running on the beach like I used to
before the cancer. I want people to remember me when I was
well, not when I was sick."

"Would you draw that for me, Anthony? I've only known
you when you've been sick. Would you show me what you
were like when you were well?"

"Sure! But would you tell me more about your father, Dr.
Bill?"

"I will, but will you tell me more about how you feel about your battle with cancer? Would you be willing to draw me a picture of that?"

"Tomorrow, when you come see me again, I will have a picture of me and my cancer."

"Fair enough. Now let me tell you about my father."

He listened intently as I described my father's life and battle with a rare disease, and how, as a fifteen-year-old, I made the commitment to care for him until his death. Anthony had many questions, and eventually, he began to understand that my relationship with my father was more important than dwelling upon his impending death. Death could never take away the love my father and I had for each other.

"Dr. Bill, I already have a drawing of me and my cancer. But I was afraid to show it to anyone. I think I can now." He pulled out of his dresser drawer a picture. I asked him to describe it for me.

"This is a picture of a rocket that is just about to crash into a fiery mass of destruction, hurting all those near it."

"I see five people nearby. Is that your mom, dad, and your sister? Who are the other two?"

"My grandparents."

"And the rocket is you, isn't it?"

"Yes. My cancer isn't just killing me, but it's destroying everyone near me. We were all so happy until I got cancer. It's all my fault!"

Then Anthony leaned against me and wept. And wept. He hadn't cried like this ever before. He felt so responsible for all the sadness and anguish his family was having to endure.

The next day, I called for a family conference and I asked

Anthony to share his picture. I told them no one was to leave, no matter how emotional things got to be, and it was indeed a very emotional time. But they listened to him, and Anthony felt they had listened. They talked about their journey with this disease that had attacked their son, their brother, their grandson. They told the truth. For the first time, everyone was telling each other the truth. It was a marathon session, and we would have more of them from time to time so they would stay committed to the honesty this nine-year-old said he needed from them.

The last drawing Anthony gave to me was a picture of the ocean with the sun on the horizon. It was a beautiful and colorful picture. And flying around in the sky were five birds all clustered together.

"Are the birds your family, Anthony? And is the sun setting a symbol of you?"

"Yes and no, Dr. Bill. You forget I'm from New Jersey, and unlike here in California, the sun rises on the ocean's horizon."

"No more rockets crashing, huh, Anthony?"

"No more crashing rockets, Dr. Bill. I'm into sunrises."

Anthony would go home after the trial of new medications. He would die before the end of that year. I often go to the beach to watch the sun set into the ocean, and I always think about a nine-year-old boy who taught me so much about the attitude of living with adversity.

A LOVE STORY UNSPOKEN

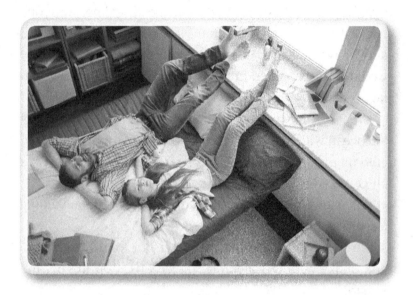

Carolyn was just sixteen. She had an advanced form of cancer that was weakening her more every day. Alan was twenty-three. His cancer was just as advanced and was also weakening his ability to thrive. Carolyn was from the deep South; Alan was from New York City. Carolyn had two very committed and protective parents, and Alan was alone and had no support system.

They came to try an experimental cancer treatment regimen they hoped would give them more time. But, by the time they arrived, the doctors had told them their cancer was too far along and they would not be accepted as candidates to participate in the drug trials. Unfortunately, they were both so weak it was necessary to keep them in the hospital and provide them with palliative care. That's when I was called in to assist them and Carolyn's family. Their rooms were on the same floor and hallway.

Initially, both of them were able to get out of bed, and with wheelchairs, they were able to leave their rooms. They met each other in the hall as their wheelchairs gently ran into each other. It was love at first sight. For the next two weeks, they were nearly inseparable. They ate together, spent long hours in the patients' lounge, sat together at the end of the hall, and looked out of windows that displayed a beautiful ocean and sunsets.

I would meet with them individually each day. But all they wanted to talk about was each other. They were deliriously happy, and each felt deeply for the other, which included a strong spiritual connection. They could each sense what the other was thinking, feeling, and hoping. Talking was often unnecessary because they could both sense what the other would say. They would tell me this consistently, and I would validate it with the other. It was a form of love one rarely sees.

Carolyn's parents were struggling with this relationship. They wanted Carolyn to be happy in the midst of the peril she was facing. But they also didn't want her to possibly endure the feelings that might come should the relationship come to an end. They wanted to protect her from the pain and emotional upheaval a love relationship can sometimes bring. They knew this would only weaken her even more.

In a special session with Carolyn and her parents, she explained what would eventually help both of them to be put at ease. Carolyn said, "I never thought I would ever know love as you two know love. But Alan has given me a chance to get just a sense of what it must be like to love someone so deeply. We will never make love. We will never have a wedding, and, Daddy, I have dreams of you walking me down the aisle. Alan and I will never be able to have children or give you grandchildren. But our love for one another is so genuine, so sincere, we truly believe God is with us and for us. Mom, Dad, we want your blessing. We want you to share in our joy."

Alan would bring his own understanding of the relationship. He would, in a counseling session, say, "I don't know what to do! I didn't ever expect to fall in love with someone. I don't know how this happened. For so long, I would wake up, and the first thing I would think about is that I have cancer and it's killing me. The last thing I would think about before I went to sleep at night is that I have cancer and it's killing me. But now, Carolyn is the first and last thing I think about every day. I want so much to live as long as I possibly can because I don't want to lose even one moment of life with her. I know many will judge us and consider our relationship to be nothing more than a distraction from our fight with cancer. I also know we will never be able to experience what it means to be a couple. But I do know that I truly love Carolyn and she truly loves me. We both believe there will be a life eternal and we will be together."

Carolyn and Alan would eventually be discharged from the hospital but would remain at the clinic for further treatment. They saw each other every day, but they had agreed to be sure that Carolyn's family and friends would also be given time to be together. Eventually, I was able to bring them all in for counseling, and it wasn't long before the four of them were regularly together. Alan had no family, but Carolyn's parents began to realize they had anough room in their lives to "adopt" Alan into the family, and Alan accepted.

I continued to provide them counseling, but the cancer was winning. Both were so weak they were readmitted to the hospital and placed in a special wing of the facility that I had been asked to create: seven beds dedicated to those who would die. Every staff member had been given special training, including the woman who emptied the trash. Everyone on this wing had volunteered to be a part of an experiment to create an environment to support patients and their families at a very dramatic moment—the time of death. In fact, it came to be known, unofficially, as the death ward.

Carolyn was admitted first, but Alan was admitted two days later. I asked they be placed in adjacent rooms. They wanted to be in the same room, but hospital protocol would not permit it. Both were were so weak they couldn't get out of bed, and both were on oxygen support. Carolyn's family and Alan had agreed to no longer fight the cancer. They had elected to only receive pain medication. They weren't even eating any longer. Water and glycerin swabs were the only things they were being given. They became the talk of the hospital. Two lovers, coming to the end of life. Each thinking only of the welfare of the other.

"Is Alan taking his pain medication? Is he still able to take it in a cocktail? Tell him I'm not going to be awake much longer. I'm so tired, and my time is soon. I sense it's soon for him too. Please, go be with him, Dr. Stephenson. I don't want him to die alone, and he has no one else but us and you. Tell him I will be waiting for him on the other side."

I went next door and found Alan barely able to talk. "I'm on my way. I don't even feel like I'm here anymore. Tell C I will be waiting for her with open arms on the other side. Go. I want to be alone. I want to be with C."

I went back to Carolyn's room, and her parents were in tears. Carolyn had just died. I stayed with them for a while and then went back to Alan's room. The nurses were all around him. The doctor had just pronounced Alan's time of death.

I remain convinced Alan and Carolyn were close and together in life, in death, and in life after death. I even think they planned the end. They were so in tune with each other they knew how to go out together. I was able to witness two people who were deeply in love but unable to truly express it because of her age and because of their health. Yet they would capture the imagination of those around them. It was truly a love story unspoken.

GRATITUDE*

When it seems
all before me is dark,
I need to remember
so it seemed to many
who have gone on before me.
When mistrust and doubt are upon me;
and I am battling despair,
I need to remember
the great and good
of every time
have had to find their way,
as I must,
by their courage
and in confidence and trust.
I need to remember to keep close company
with their spirits.

*This poem is dedicated to all my clients who entrusted me to
be with them and counsel them in the last days of their lives.

A MAN WHO WAS
FED UP WITH HIMSELF

I was flying up to Seattle to see a client. Seated next to me was a man who had apparently waited for the plane to depart while in the bar because he was ready to talk. When he discovered I was a psychotherapist, he paused and said, "I think I really want to talk with you." And then he poured out his pain. He told me about his failure in marriage . . . all three of them. He talked about his conflicts at work with his colleagues and how he had let his children down and the things he did and wished he had not done.

After more than two hours of intense conversation he put his hand on my arm and said, "Dr. Stephenson, you don't know how much I hate myself."

We soon parted after exiting the plane, but the memory of that statement stayed with me. I suspect most of us can recall saying something like this. There are still others who say that about themselves over and over again. The hardest approval to get is our own.

Renowned Austrian psychotherapist, Dr. Alfred Adler, said that the fear of being left out, the fear of being ignored, of being insignificant, is one of the deepest fears we humans have. It is the momentum behind the drive to feel important, to be important.

Abraham Maslow, a psychiatrist, in his autobiography recalls working with a young college student when he himself was a young counselor. The student came to him and poured out his feelings of worthlessness and how he felt he wasn't worthy to live.

Maslow said, "I couldn't really believe anyone could feel that about himself and so I didn't take him seriously." But two days later, the student shot himself.

It wasn't that he shot himself that turned Dr. Maslow toward a new understanding of the pain as well as the potential in human beings. It was where he did it. The student had gone out to the city dump and stood on top of a garbage heap, and there he shot himself. As if to say, "This is all that I'm worth."

Seldom will our feelings of worthlessness and self-hate be that dramatically displayed, but we're no strangers to it either. Every one of us fights with that feeling of being insignificant, unimportant, or undeserving of any love or respect.

How much can we change? We know people can change when they hurt enough; when they get tired of the direction they're going in; when there's no longer any satisfaction for them in what they're doing. It's painful and they get fed up with that pain.

This is the model for the Twelve Step program. The most important part of change is discovering or believing in the possibility that we can change.

Recovery comes when we learn to let go of the foolish expectations we have about ourselves. Recovery comes when we no longer feel the need to pressure other people to love us. Then we can seize and hold on to the fact we are already loved, understood, forgiven, and accepted by a Higher Power. Freedom from our addictive-self begins there. Freedom from the pain of self-loathing can be found there as well.

CONFINEMENT

I feel the clashes going on within.
I am battling the very nature of my being
The good versus the bad
The best of me versus the worst of me
The coward versus the brave
The kindliness versus my meanness.

There is a part of me that I admire in my enemy
and dislike in my friends.
There is this battle going on inside of me
and when someone confronts me with my
hypocrisy, I feel exposed, shame and resentment.

It is then I know I am seeking
validation in the wrong place.
It is then I know I am seeking
to be my own savior.

O soul,
I need to remind myself what I often counsel.
I will know true freedom when instead of using
the days of my years and
the energies of my life
trying to get approval from others

I do the tasks I know I was called to do:
To do justice
To love mercy
To step into the lives of the wounded
To walk humbly with my God.

Then I am free.
Indeed.

CHRISTAL WITH AN "I"

She was just twelve years old. Her name was Christal. I kept using a "y" but she insisted on the "i." I used to tease her about that. It was our way of finding something to smile about. She would then tell me my name should be a "v" instead of a "ph." But I insisted on the "ph." And then we would start thinking of other names we could play this game with.

She was dying. I would be the family therapist for the six short weeks I came to know them. Christal had cystic fibrosis, some retardation, and had battled pneumonia on a regular basis. It would kill her eventually.

Christal came from a very poor family. They couldn't afford the expensive medical care she needed, including a therapist. I'm not cheap, but sometimes I am free. Her family ended up declaring bankruptcy and sold their house. All to give Christal the care they wanted for their daughter.

They are amazing parents.

Christal's main issue was she knew she would never make it to thirteen; to be a teenager. She wanted the symbol a teen represented versus what a child represented. She was grieving over what could not be, not what she was dealing with physically.

Christal was also feeling guilty because she knew the financial bind the family was in because of her illness. She worried that her parents would not be able to afford new oxygen tanks or the breathing medicine.

One night, she asked me to come and sit with her because she was unable to get to sleep and she was afraid she couldn't breathe if she fell asleep, even though she was on oxygen 24/7. In the dark, I sat and together we breathed.

I asked her, "Christal, when you are in bed alone at night, how do you slow your breathing so you can go to sleep?"

She said, "I look out my window at all of the stars. I then start naming them after all the people who have helped me and have loved me. But I always run out of stars." And, we began to name the stars that night until she fell asleep.

When there is so little time, I become deeply attached to my clients and their family. Christal was no exception. I would see her and her parents nearly every day. There were good days and scary days. She was in and out of the hospital on a regular basis, trying to manage her bouts with pneumonia.

I had to go away for eight days. It had been planned before I came to know her, and she knew I was going to be gone. She encouraged me to go because she knew I needed some time with my family; she valued family very much. She said she would still be there when I got back. But while I was gone, I checked in daily: her status was worsening. She was in hospice care, and they thought it would be very soon.

I returned and immediately went to her bedside. I said, "Hi, Christal with a 'y.'"

She said, "Hi, Dr. Stephenson with a 'v.'" I sat, and we just looked at each other. Every breath was so painful for her. She said from behind her oxygen mask, "I waited for you."

Tears in my eyes, I said, "I love you, Christal with an 'i.'"

"I love you, Dr. Stephenson with a 'ph.'"

She would die late that night with parents, grandparents, and myself in the background. Early the next morning, as her parents and I were having coffee together in the hospital cafe, they said, "Dr. Stephenson, we have decided to take all of the memorial money and give it to the Cystic Fibrosis Foundation, and we also plan to be speakers to support this cause. We want other parents to know they are not alone."

I smiled and knew they didn't need me any longer. They were on their way. They were broke and deeply in debt, and yet they were full of hope. No, they didn't need me anymore. My work was done.

UNTITLED

I listen for the Voice that speaks to me in my quietness.
I look to the Light that shines in my darkness.
I seek a sense of Presence that fills my emptiness
and reveals the Mystery that gives me meaning.
A Meaning that penetrates my mystery.

O soul,
remind me that I am a precious child of God
who knows me by name
and loves me with grace.

O soul,
the tremors are out of control tonight.
Teach me to be still and open to the
calm and grace I invite to embrace.

A DAY OF FULFILLMENT

I come to this sacred place and time
full of much that
clutters and distracts
stifles and burdens
making me a burden
to others
to myself.

I come to this sacred place and time
to empty me
of gnawing dissatisfactions
of anxious imaginings

of nagging resentment
of old scores to settle.

I come to this sacred place and time
to empty me of the arrogance
of always having to be right
secure and safe
in a world that God fills
with so many surprises.

I come to this sacred place and time
to be filled with
not only peace and contentment
but with hope and confidence.

I come to this sacred place and time
with a passion and commitment
to bring my will
into harmony with God's will.

That the best is yet to be.

ON HOLY GROUND

I was visiting a client who was in the hospital to undergo an experimental treatment for her advanced form of cancer. We had become good friends, and toward the end of our session we were laughing and having a good time.

Evidently, a patient in the adjoining room had overheard our conversation about how to live until we die, and she asked the nurse if I would come and visit her after I was finished with my client.

I want to pause and paint a picture of the patient I walked in to meet. Day and night she had to have an oxygen tube in her nostrils in order to stay alive. The cancer was in both lungs, and she was slowly suffocating to death. The cancer was also in her bones and joints and back, and she was in constant pain, even though she was heavily medicated. Every movement was agony for her.

This lady would die in this tiny room, alone. Seldom, if ever, did anyone ever come to visit or offer her a word of comfort. She said, "They don't know what to say, and they can't bear watching me in such pain."

This woman's mind, however, was as sharp as any mind I knew. This woman's spirit was more lovely than any flower arrangement or any symphony of an orchestra. I sensed that I was in the presence of a teacher and my soul was about to be enriched.

I sat down with her, and we talked. She said, "I need to talk to someone who will listen, and I believe you are the one to do that."

"Yes, ma'am. I will listen, but from time to time, I want to tell you what I hear you saying. Deal?"

"Deal."

For over an hour, this woman would talk about her life, her family, and her faith. She told me what she was proud of and what she was ashamed of. At the end of the hour, we were both exhausted.

As I prepared to leave, I said, "Mamie, before I go, can I tell you a joke?"

Her eyes lit up, and I told her a joke. It was funny. I'm not going to tell you the joke, but it was very funny.

And then she said, "Dr. Stephenson, can I tell you a joke?"

She told me one, and it too was very funny. We both laughed. There was a moment when I felt as if my soul was at one with her soul. There, in that room of death, a seasoned psychotherapist and a cancer-stricken lady, both of us surrounded by the smells of disinfectant and death, giggling like two kids caught with their hands in the cookie jar!

When we finished laughing, we paused and just looked at each other in silence for several moments. I leaned over and gave her a kiss on her cheek, and then she kissed me. It was a sacred moment. I felt like I wanted to take off my shoes because I knew I was standing on holy ground. We were never to see each other again.

WHERE DO I GO?

As I sit here in the cold, dampness
  that is in my life, I realize
  I have lost the joy
  I had in my life
  I once had inside me . . .
  The hope I had in tomorrow . . .

Gone.

I am so completely alone.

I need my soul to kiss me again
  to touch me with tenderness

warm and wet upon my skin
and whisper in my heart
the claim upon me,
the claim life has upon me.

In my wider world . . .
so dark and weary . . .
a mystery without an answer . . .
my thoughts reach out
with trembling fingers into the
vastness before me,
grasping at life's larger meaning.
The faces of those who wait for me
overwhelm my capacity to give what they need
and I am lost in their pleas.

O soul,
if I could just learn
to kiss the joy
as it flies, as it flies . . .

(Author's note: This poem's title and content came from a sixteen-year-old who was in an advanced stage of cancer with parents constantly fighting.)

WHO DO YOU LISTEN TO?

"**It's impossible,**" said Pride.
"**It's risky,**" said Experience.
"**It's pointless,**" said Reason.
"**Give it a try,**" whispered my heart.

UNCONQUERED LOVE

Erin and Rick were going to be married. They were in their early twenties. But then, the unexpected happened. Rick was in a horrible automobile accident. He had extensive head injuries, and the doctors pronounced him dead on arrival.

However, one doctor decided to check for a pulse one last time. He was surprised to find a very faint one. This is their story.

Rick was in a coma for more than three months. His mother had been told on a number of occasions that he had only a few hours left to live. She refused to resign to that prognosis, as did Erin. Every night, Erin was at his bedside, talking to him as if it was just another normal day. She would talk to him like they were out on a date as if nothing had happened several months before. Each night, at the close of her time with him, she would recite Psalm 23, "The Lord is my shepherd. . . . "

One night, a doctor on duty spoke to Erin. "Miss Anderson, you are young and pretty, and you should start thinking about going out and having fun and try to forget Rick. He will never walk or talk again. He will never be the same as before." Erin refused to listen, and she would never abandon him. And again, to medicate the sting of the doctor's judgment, she recited, "The Lord is my shepherd. . . . "

One day, Rick opened his eyes. But he couldn't speak or move. Erin continued by his side every night. She decorated his room for Halloween and then Thanksgiving and then Christmas.

On New Year's Eve, she decorated his room with crepe paper and balloons.

Erin said, "I put a hat on Rick, and at the stroke of midnight I blew horns and told him the new year was here. The nurses thought I was crazy, talking to a man who was not much more than a vegetable. But I sensed that Rick could hear me and understand. I looked into his eyes, and I recited to him, "The Lord is our shepherd. . . . "

Rick's recovery was slow and painful. He was being called the "miracle boy" in the hospital. But movement began to return. At first, it was just a finger. And then an arm, and then a leg. But when he tried to talk, only a gutteral sound could be uttered.

Later, Rick said, "I could only mumble. No one understood me except Erin. She knew and understood everything I would try to say."

Eventually, Rick was discharged to home. Erin quit her job to help Rick's mother take care of him. She withdrew her savings and bought an outdoor pool so that Rick could exercise his legs. As she was withdrawing all of her savings, she recited, "The Lord is my shepherd. . . . "

Throughout that year, Rick worked hard with a speech therapist, and he began to get his speech back. So much so that he went to Erin's father and said, "Sir, I would like permission to ask Erin to marry me."

It would be another year of hard work, but with Erin's help, on their wedding day, Rick was able, with a walker, to walk down the aisle of the church and turn and stand, proudly upright, as Erin and her father began their entrance.

Erin said, "As I was walking down the aisle, I looked at Rick, and silently I began to say from my heart, "The Lord is my shepherd. I shall not want; he makes me lie down in green pastures. He leads me beside still waters; he restores my soul. He leads me in paths of righteousness for his name's sake. Even though I walk through the valley of darkness, I fear no evil; for thou art with me; thy rod and thy staff, they comfort me. Thou preparest a table before me in the presence of my enemies; thou anointest my head with oil, my cup overflows. Surely goodness and mercy shall follow me all the days of my life, and I shall dwell in the house of the Lord forever."

It was a wedding filled with victory, hope, and unconquered love.

CONSCIENCE

Let me off
from the world
and my share of its evils.
Let me off.

Let me off
from the claim that injustices
make upon me.
Let me off.

Let me off
from the evil I condone
and the momentous needs I refuse to notice.
Let me off.
O soul,
It's not within me.

(Author's note: Assisting persons who are coming to the end
of life has its consequences. The challenge is to cope with and
care for the grief that comes with the loss as well as the grief
that I witness from families and friends. This poem is just a
way to vent that pressure.)

WHAT ARE YOU IN FOR?

I am convinced that the cruelest form of punishment is having to eat alone. We often use it with those who can no longer independently participate in the community such as a church or synagogue.

"What did you do wrong?"

"Arthritis and a broken hip. I'm unable to get out of the house."

"Yeah, that'll do it."

"And you, what did you do?"

"My husband died, and I'm eighty-six."

"Aha! That serves you right!"

Two stories.

I was asked to provide counseling to two women who were both diagnosed as being terminally ill. Both women were widows, and both of them lived alone. These women taught me to understand the power of inclusiveness.

Mrs. Henderson. Terminally ill and living in a skilled nursing facility. Beautiful place. Lots of visitor parking spaces, but not one car using them. I found her room, and the staff eventually wheeled her into the area I was to use to conduct the interview.

The first thing I said was, "What are you in for?"

She said, "Talking to myself."

"Ah! That'll do it."

Apparently, she belonged to a large church with several ministers, choirs, fellowship groups, and several women's groups, Bible classes, and groups that take trips.

"How long has it been since anybody from your church came to visit, Mrs. Henderson?"

"You're the first person to come visit me since my husband's funeral in over three months, and you're not even from the church."

Punishment for getting sick and talking to herself. Make her eat alone.

Another client, Mrs. Rollins. A woman in her mid-seventies, living in a beautiful home overlooking the Los Angeles basin. She now lived alone since her husband had died. On the mantel were pictures of all her kids and grandchildren who apparently lived on the East Coast. All too busy to come and visit.

She said, "Sit down and relax. I'll go and fix us some lunch. It won't take long."

I hadn't planned on eating. But after several minutes, I got restless sitting there all alone, so I went looking for her. She had a large formal dining room that could seat over a dozen at the table, which was beautifully adorned with the finest of china and linens with creases two inches deep.

I said, "Mrs. Rollins, we could have just as easily eaten in the kitchen." But she kept at it. Cloth napkins in silver rings. Stemmed crystal ware. Beautiful silverware. Candles in silver candlesticks.

"Mrs. Rollins, there's no need for all this formality."

"Dr. Stephenson, my doctor told me why you're here. Will you please be quiet and sit down?"

"Yes, ma'am, I was going to do that next."

She said, "Apparently, you don't know what it's like to fix a meal for one."

"No, ma'am, I don't."

She and I sat at her beautiful dining room table together, and we had a banquet. There were many of us that day. She assured me that the number around the table that day was twice as many as she had had in months and months and months.

I would be going to see both women on a regular basis, but always when it was time to eat. It would not be long before their cancer became so overwhelming that they could not host or eat with me. But there were stories. They kept repeating the times we sat and ate together.

A LOVE STORY

Kathy would be one of my earliest of terminally ill clients. She was twenty-nine, and I was thirty-one. Her cancer was Hodgkin's lymphoma. Even though cancer had ravaged her body, she was still a very attractive woman and had an internal spirit that was even more beautiful.

She was single and from Santa Barbara, but she was down in the San Diego area, at a cancer clinic that was known to treat patients from all over the world who had been told to go home and live until they died because there was nothing else that could be done for them. I was in charge of an experimental program that was then known as the death ward. The death ward consisted of seven beds in the hospital section of the facility for persons too sick to go to the clinic or be moved back home. I also did extensive counseling for other clients at the clinic of the hospital, and this is where I came to know Kathy.

Because my clients would not live very long, I rarely saw a client for counseling longer than three months. But Kathy would become an exception. Kathy staved off death for almost a year and, in so doing, became one of my longest counseling clients.

Through counseling, Kathy came to make peace with her estranged parents, her brother, and even with her cancer. While she was in remission, she decided to be a volunteer at the clinic where she was receiving outpatient treatment and helped new people at the clinic become more acclimated to the clinic's surroundings. Many of the patients were coming from foreign countries and from nearly every state in the union. Kathy became the most popular patient on the campus. She had found purpose.

I could sense that Kathy was in love with me. It's quite common for a client to transfer her feelings to the one who is giving her so much support. I began to examine my own feelings and sensed counter-transference might have been adding to the dynamic. I, too, was single and cared deeply for Kathy. Perhaps too deeply.

Three months passed. I kept my guard up and continued giving her counseling as we avoided the elephant in the room. The doctors then told her there was nothing more they could do for her. She needed to go home. Her prognosis was one to three months.

Kathy looked exhausted, and she was in a lot of pain, but she returned to Santa Barbara and promised to stay in touch with me daily. When she was leaving, I could tell she wanted to kiss me, but I kept to my boundaries, even though I had my own desire. I sensed we would never see each other again.

Two months passed. Kathy called nearly every day. When she knew she had a week or less to live, she asked me to come up to Santa Barbara to be with her until she died. I agreed.

She lived in a luxurious home that overlooked the ocean and Santa Barbara. Kathy was surrounded by family, friends, and caregivers. Her brother had taken over the duties of being her primary caregiver.

I met with Kathy at least twice a day. She was unable to endure any more than fifteen-to-twenty-minute sessions because the pain was so intense. In working with her prescribing nurse, her morphine cocktail was increased to Q4R, which meant she would get the pain medication every four hours around the clock even if she wasn't in significant pain. But it was only a partial victory. Kathy had a very low threshold for pain, and thus the comfort from the increase in morphine was only temporary.

On the fourth day, Kathy called me into her room. She wanted to end this suffering, for herself as well as for those who loved her. We both knew this included me. We couldn't look at each other without communicating how much we cared for each other. I asked her how I could help. She asked if I would help her inject enough morphine that would end her life and her suffering.

I brought her brother into the room, and the three of us discussed her request to die. He agreed that assisting her to die was the right thing to do. Kathy and I injected her IV drip with a large dose of morphine. We sat together on the side of her bed and waited for the morphine to take effect.

She said, "Bill, I'm in love with you, and I know you are in love with me. Thank you for the way you have loved me this past year. Can we kiss goodbye?"

It was a long, deep, and passionate kiss. Both of us were in tears. She took a quick breath and collapsed in my arms. The morphine would compromise her respiratory system, and in minutes Kathy stopped breathing. I held her close and wept until her brother pulled her from my arms.

Her brother and I bathed and dressed her for her funeral. There was no need for her hair to be done. She didn't have any. It was a good death. But it's one of the few that I remember every year—the date of death, June 29, when I pause and remember her. There is a part of me that believes she remains in my soul and gently guides my way with the many others who would follow her.

CHAPTER TWO
THE COURAGE TO CHANGE

AS I BEGIN AGAIN

As I begin this new day,
I yearn to see and hear
as God bids the earth to turn
and the sun to shine.

God speaks and creation sings
in spontaneous chorus,
unfurling flowers flag my attention.

As I begin again,
I will open my senses to the wonder of this day.
Its wild freshness and newness nudge me,
its ode to joy pulls and pushes me along,
its intimate loveliness invades my thinking,
its beauty breathes hope into my soul.

A GOOD BEGINNING

We are a child-centered society, and we put a great emphasis on educating our children because we believe our children should have a good beginning. A good beginning should never be underestimated. But it may be the fact we are estimating it so much that this will be the child's biggest danger. It may be in thinking that a good beginning will provide a good ending we have failed to see the greatest temptations in life come not in adolescence but in maturity.

While at my fiftieth college reunion, I was talking with one of my classmates and we were reminiscing about mutual friends and we centered on one we had both known. He had all of the things many of us envied. He was not only an achiever but a super achiever. The one behind whose name everyone would write in the yearbook, "The future holds great promise for you."

But then, at the pinnacle of his career, a failure set into his life, and in response to that failure he went down into his basement and shot himself.

Most of us have known persons like him. Educated to be a success but unable to handle a failure. Taught how to be independent but not knowing how to be dependent, and in their maturity, they go to pieces.

We are taught all our lives to be successful . . . to make our mark . . . to make a contribution. We are told that in this world the awards are not handed out to the helpless. You've got to be somebody to be an achiever, a winner. But if that's all we are taught, then we are not being taught one of the greatest truths about life. The truth is that at the beginning and end we are most vulnerable and dependent on others. To accept and embrace this part of our life story is a sign of strength and wellness.

THE CONSEQUENCES OF ANGER

Not too long ago, divers recovered a German U-boat off Denmark that had been sunk by the Allies in WWII. But it was too dangerous to get close to or to enter because there were still live torpedoes on board capable of blowing up. The war is over, but that German sub is still armed for battle.

I had a client who was a teenager, and he lived in a home like that. Anger flared up. There was a fight, and the home was turned into a battlefield. Then a truce was made. That's all. Just a cessation of hostility. The heat of the anger still smoldered. There was no real reconciliation, no real recovery. There was no true peace restored.

The war was over, but the home was still occupied with live torpedoes. Occupants of the house had to walk gingerly so as not to step on somebody's feelings or else there would be another explosion. And my client asked, "Dr. Stephenson, what can I do? Where can I go?"

He was also battling fourth stage cancer. When he died in the hospital, he chose to avoid the dangerous waters by not having his parents with him. I believe he chose not to die in a war zone.

KINDERGARTEN

I am learning
some of the most precious moments
I have
are when I give myself and those near me

the time to listen very carefully.
Sometimes I wonder
if I live life too cautiously
share my faith too stingily
administer my commitments from a medicine dropper
make my offerings from my leftovers.

Too often I live
from a frightened spirit
rather than a generous heart.
Why do I choose to live my life out of a scarcity concept?
I give of myself to others as if I have to give up something.

I am learning
that I give as I receive.
When I feel abundant love and abundant grace,
then I give the same way.
I give to others from an expression of my compassion.

I need to remember
that the only thing I take beyond the grave
is what I release before I go there.

EXPECTING CHANGE

Hope, but never expect. Look forward, but never wait.

I was asked to work with a small community in the northwest to prepare them for the death of a significant and highly respected member of this small town. It was an unusual assignment to be given. To counsel a whole community in grief recovery. Add to that was the participation of the patient.

One day, I was sitting in the local coffee shop, having breakfast, and staring at this man in a wheelchair. He could move his head and parts of his fingers but nothing else. He had a man-servant who cut up his food and placed it on a special mechanically powered fork that he would use to eat.

He saw me staring at him and invited me to join him at his table. His name was Stephen. He knew who I was and why I was in his town. For several hours we sat at that table and we got to know each other on a deeply personal level. I never knew a man who was more radiant, more relevant, more energizing to talk and get to know than Stephen. We would end up spending two days together, developing a rapport and trust that usually takes years to establish.

Stephen was a very successful businessman. He was in the natural gas business. Thirteen years before our encounter, when he was forty years old, he was waiting for news of a natural gas discovery to occur any moment.

He said, "I had so much nervous energy. I saw the storm clouds gathering, and I decided to clean out the gutters rather than sitting around waiting for this gas well to come in."

He climbed up the ladder to clean out the pine cones when he noticed piles of pine needles on the roof. He decided to sweep them off, and his wife handed up the broom. As he backed up, he had forgotten that several years before he had cut out a piece of the overhang of the roof to allow a little pine tree to grow through it. As he was backing down the roof, he fell through that open space. He landed on his back. He was paralyzed for the rest of his life, except for his head and his hands.

When he finished sharing his story, he knew what I was thinking. How would I handle that if it ever happened to me?

I asked him: "How do you do it all? How do you suddenly stop hiking, fishing, and running marathons?"

He said, "There are three things you have to do when something like this happens. The first thing you have to do is adjust. The second thing you do is adjust. And the third thing you do is adjust."

He said, "By adjusting to your abilities, Bill, you have to change your self-expectations. If you can't be a physical athlete any longer, then perhaps you can be a spiritual athlete." He was.

Stephen would volunteer to join my team to work with the citizens of his town to prepare for the death of the person who was "family" to them. Stephen's testimony would make this unique project a huge success.

THE ANXIETY OF CHANGE

I want to believe I can change.
  I am tired of the direction I'm going.
  I am not satisfied with what I am doing
  and the pain I am experiencing tells me
  I have got to make some changes.

I can't change
  the circumstances
  I find myself.
  But, I believe I can change my
  attitude toward those circumstances.

Where do I find the courage to separate
  myself from what other people think of me
  and become more concerned about me?

When will I stop putting pressure on other
  people in order to be loved?

When will I understand I need to stop
  loving things and using people?

I will be still.
  Take a breath.

Wait.
Wait some more.

Until I have the strength to accept
the freedom that comes with receiving a
love that will never let me go.

Then,
I will know I already have all I need.

FREEDOM FOUND

How do you talk to yourself? We all do, of course. Some of us even out loud. My wife often says, "What did you say?" or "Did you say something?" I am constantly getting caught talking to myself.

Some of us talk to ourselves by running ourselves down: "Can't you do anything right?" We become great persuaders. We convince ourselves that we can't, and our body begins to illustrate it.

Sometimes we talk to ourselves by saying, "Be on guard! Cover up! Protect yourself! Don't admit you've done anything wrong." People who say that to themselves often become rigid and stiff, and their bodies begin to show it.

Contemporary therapists are discovering that people who are under emotional pressure and stress get healthier faster when they are able to very quickly admit they made a mistake, and admit when they are wrong.

Occasionally we weaken our will when we talk to ourselves with self-pity. "You poor thing. Things are so tough for you. People are all against you. Obviously, there's a conspiracy going on against you." And we begin to weaken our will, and our body begins to believe what we tell it.

There comes a time when we weaken ourselves by talking to ourselves in such a way that we go through life blaming other people for everything that happens to us and deny we have the freedom to choose.

How do you talk to yourself? Do you blame everything that has happened to you on other people? If you do, you are giving up your freedom. Our bodies will then take that abdication of freedom and react in ways that are consequential. You can see it in the eyes, in the slump of the shoulders. Their bodies are symbols for their failures and mistakes. But, there's another way. This story.

A young husband and wife had a three-year-old son. They became my clients when after a Sunday afternoon, he was watching the football game and had a few beers. An argument ensued between him and his wife, and in a fit of anger, he stormed out of the house, got in the car, and sped out of the driveway. He did not know his three-year-old son was playing behind the car and it killed him.

What choices does this man, this couple, have in the midst of their tragedy? Do I say to them, "Well, that's not so bad . . . other people have done worse things"? That would not bring them healing and a new freedom.

Do I say to them, "From now on, you must punish yourselves enough before you die that God will forgive you." They could never do that.

Or, do I say to them, especially to him, "You will never be able to atone for this tragedy by punishing yourself or by punishing each other. But you can show your gratitude of forgiveness by reaching out and being gracious toward others."

It would take a year of counseling and sometimes painful self-examination, but an atmosphere of deep conversation, compassion, and nonjudgment enabled that word *forgiveness* to reach him, and he is now considered one of the most effective Boys Scout leaders in the world. He travels and speaks extensively to fathers everywhere how he chose to live again. How he had found freedom from his demons.

SEEKING

I seek
  a fresh breath of life into my thinking
  and a spirit into my soul.

I look
  and long for
  a new season of hope.

I have
  come to see how the evil in this world
  and the conflicts in my life

are linked to each other
and often much alike.

I struggle
   with clinging to my fears and nourishing my gloom
   with fighting the temptation to turn outward
   blaming those around me
   for all that I feel within me.

I seek
   a vessel that will transport
   the kindness and gentleness I look for
   and bring to closer fruition all the hunger
   and hope of this yearning heart.

THE FEAR OF LONELINESS

Two mysteries of life I haven't figured out. First, why, when you end up with only one scok and you throw it away, that is when the other sock shows up? I have never understood that mystery. Second, why, on an airplane, are the talkers and the non-talkers seated next to each other?

I was seated by a woman who was ready to talk. I had a lecture that needed to be refined. I had no sooner buckled my seatbelt when she turned to me and said, "I am so nervous!"

I thought she was afraid to fly, and I was wondering what word of comfort I might give to her. But, she continued, "I'm so nervous because I have to make a decision this week whether to get married the second time or not. What do you think?"

I really wanted to say, "Madam, you didn't ask me about the first time, why are you asking me about this one?" But we were still strangers and hadn't really met yet.

That didn't seem to handicap this dear lady. It is a curious thing, how we can talk about such personal things under the protection of anonymity at thirty thousand feet, and yet those same words can stick in our throat with someone we know intimately and sitting directly across the table.

She went on to wonder with me about which direction she should go. Then, she said to herself, but out loud, "Well, I suppose there are some things worse than being alone. I could be marrying someone like my first husband, who treated me horribly! There are some things worse than living alone."

And she's right! Perhaps in a deeper way than she thought. There are some things worse than being alone. There is the fear of being alone. That's worse.

The need to always have someone to talk to; the need to always have the TV on when you're by yourself; the need to always have people around you; the fear of having to face aloneness; the fear of having to listen to one's own silence, to one's own solitude.

I am more and more convinced of the therapeutic power of silence and the healing that solitude can bring to our lives. When we listen to our loneliness rather than fearing it, we discover that learning how to live with others is secondary to learning how to live with ourselves.

PERFECTION

In parts of India, where they make some of those beautiful rugs, the rug will be hanging and the artisan will be on the side of the design, while the apprentice will be on the other side. The task of the apprentice is to push the needle back in through so the artisan can continue to fill in the design. But the apprentice, like all of us, sees in a mirror dimly. He can't always see the design on the other side. Again and again, he pushes back through in the wrong place. He makes mistakes.

But the artisan doesn't turn to the apprentice and say, "You stupid man! You're fired! I'm through with you!" Rather, he has the ability to take the mistake, change the design, and weave it another way. In the end, a beautiful rug has been made.

What a parable! People who elect to be in recovery soon learn that perfection means "right purpose." We, like the apprentice, make mistakes, but we can learn from those mistakes and, like the great artisan, not give up on ourselves.

Good mental health is when we can take our failures and weave them into the design of our lives, so we can say, "Oh, how beautiful!"

A NEW BEGINNING

Let this new beginning
be a time to re-sensitize my vision.
To give me rest and renewal.
To be refreshed and know
I can begin again.
To be touched and felt with the
forgiveness I can embrace.

As I live through this new beginning,
I will fight off any self-pity in my loss,
any fear of what is to come.

Let the legacy of my memories
of having been loved
speak through my actions
of goodwill and caring for others

To embrace the challenge
to be open
to change, and to tomorrow.
To a new way of living.
To reach out to others
with the quiet and confidence of faith.

To not add to the hopelessness
of anyone who comes in my midst.

I will live with what I
embrace in this new beginning.
To touch others with God's grace
and find joy again.

PERCEIVING OUR CIRCUMSTANCES

How do you judge your day? Each of us has personal, private, and sometimes very secret circumstances that could color our day. Some circumstances can be so cruel, so ugly, they ride high, wide, and unhandsome across our dearest hopes and dreams and leave us empty and wanting. Circumstances can crush people. They do matter.

There's an old Chinese proverb about a farmer who lived in a small country village. He was regarded as well-to-do because he had one horse and he could use that horse for both plowing and transportation.

One day, the horse ran away, and all the neighbors came and consoled him for his unfortunate circumstances. The farmer replied, "How do you know they are unfortunate?"

The next day his horse returned, bringing two wild horses with him. Those same neighbors came to congratulate him for his good circumstances. The farmer said, "How do you know these are good circumstances?"

The next day, his only son tried to ride one of those wild horses and was thrown and broke his leg. His neighbors again came to console him due to his unfortunate circumstances. The wise farmer said, "How do you know these are unfortunate circumstances?"

The next day the country went to war. Every able-bodied young man was drafted to fight, but because his son had a broken leg, he didn't have to go. His neighbors again came to him to congratulate him on his good fortune, on his good circumstances. The farmer said again, "How do you know? How do you know?"

We don't. We may think the worst thing has happened or the best thing has happened. We don't know enough about that circumstance for us to become a pessimist or an optimist.

I am learning, and I am also teaching to others, to not let circumstances define us.

JUSTIFICATION

How do I justify
my agenda for living?

How do I determine
between what may be so urgent
and what's important?

How do I decide
the difference between what may be expedient
and what is essential?

How do I make those decisions?

It is this realization
that causes me to commit to someone
who is in such despair.

To reach out and take hold of them
and assure them they will
no longer face their fears alone.

STONES OF RESENTMENT—A FABLE*

I have counseled so many couples in crisis, often blaming one another for the pain they are experiencing. This pain turns into resentment. How can a couple with so much resentment recover and find their way together again? The following parable was written by Lewis Smedes*.

Once upon a time, there was a little village called Fakin in a small country called Friezland, and in that little village lived a man named Fredrick. Fredrick was not only the village baker, he was also a very righteous man. Fredrick was so righteous it seemed as if he almost dripped righteousness from his lips. Consequently, people preferred to avoid him.

Fredrick was not only a righteous man but a married one. While Fredrick was tall and thin, his wife, Frieda, was short and round. They were opposites, not just in size, but also in temperament. Not just in posture, but also in personality. Frieda did not hold people at bay with self-righteousness. Indeed, with her warmth, she seemed to invite people into her life.

Frieda respected her husband's righteousness and she also loved him, as much as he allowed himself to be loved. But there was an ache in Frieda's heart. She wanted more warmth from him than his worthy righteousness would allow. And there lay the seat of sadness.

Late one morning, after he had been working before early dawn, preparing the dough for the oven at the bakery, Fredrick came home unexpectedly to find a stranger in the bedroom with his wife.

Frieda's adultery became the talk of the local tavern and the scandal in all the village social circles. Everybody was convinced that Fredrick would cast her out of the house because he was such a righteous man. But Fredrick surprised them all. He didn't cast Frieda out. He kept her as his wife, saying he had forgiven her. But in his heart of hearts, Fredrick could not really forgive Frieda because he thought she had brought shame to his name.

Indeed, every time he thought about her, his feelings would turn to anger and hatred and resentment. He began to look at her as a tramp, and when it came right down to it he despised her for betraying him after he had been such a good and faithful husband to her. He only pretended to forgive her. He really wanted her around so he could punish her and in some kind of twisted way "redeem" her with his mercy. On the outside, Fredrick looked and talked righteously, but inside he was seething with resentment.

Fredrick's phony forgiveness did not sit well in Heaven. Consequently, every time Fredrick felt this secret hatred toward Frieda, his Guardian Angel would drop a little pebble in Fredrick's heart. Each time he showed his resentment toward Frieda, another pebble would be dropped into his heart and he would feel this sharp stab of pain. Strangely enough, the pain he would feel felt a great deal like the pain he first felt when he saw Frieda feeding on the love of a stranger's heart. This made him hate her even more. And his hate brought more pain and his pain more hate.

Over time, the pebbles piled up until Fredrick's heart became heavy with the weight of it all. In fact, so heavy, the top part of his body began to bend forward and he had to strain his head up just to look straight ahead. He became so weary of the pain, so heavy in his heart over it all, he finally came to the place where he wished to God he was dead.

One night, the angel who was dropping the pebbles of pain into Fredrick's heart came to Fredrick and said: "There is one way in which you can be healed of this hurt. There is one remedy and one remedy only in which you can heal that which is hurting you. What you need is the miracle of magic eyes. You need a new way of looking at Frieda. Not as a wicked woman who has betrayed and hurt you, but to see her as a frightened, lonely woman who needs you. You see her with those new eyes, and a pebble will be lifted each time from your heart."

"How do I get those eyes?" Fredrick asked.

"Only ask! And desiring while you ask, they will be given to you," the angel answered.

At first, Fredrick didn't ask for these new eyes because he had come to cherish his hatred and hurt. But finally, the pain of those pebbles in his heart, the weight and the weariness of it all, drove him to ask for those new eyes, and, like they were promised, he was given them.

Fredrick began to look at Frieda in a new way, and slowly Frieda began to change before his eyes. Amazingly so! And as he began to look at her in a new way, one-by-one, a pebble was taken from his heart. Not all at once, because it had taken a long time for all that pain and hurt to build up. But as the pebbles began to be taken from his heart, he felt lighter and lighter and he began to walk more upright and he was less foreboding. He invited Frieda into his heart, and she accepted, and the two of them began to journey into the second season of humble joy.

I remind my clients, that whether or not the other person deserves forgiveness, God knows they deserve to get rid of that pain. Whatever forgiveness does for the person who did the hurting, what forgiveness will do for the one who was hurt is to give their guardian angel permission to release them from the resentment. It will give them life again. They are safe to love again. And that's what causes the guardian angels in Heaven to sing.

*From the book, *The Art of Forgiving,* by Lewis Smedes, Ballantine Press.

AS MY DAY BEGINS

As my day begins
 I will learn to grow
  into my commitments.

So
 they will be too strong
  to tolerate injustice in my thinking.

So
 I will be too honest
  to tamper with truth in my loving.

So
I will be too helpful
to be lenient with evil.

As my day begins
I will seek to have
an inner balance

So
I will forever outweigh forgiveness to the
blame that I have cast on others.

So
I save the sharpest
thrust of conscience for myself.

So
there will be
no malice, bitterness, or revenge left in me.

CHAPTER THREE
RECOVERY WITH OTHERS

I WAS WRONG

I have spent a lifetime
trying to find meaning in my life.

I thought my work
would give meaning to my life.

I thought providing counseling to people in distress
would give me meaning.

I was wrong.

The meaning isn't in the work
if it isn't, first of all, in the person.

I thought by seeking happiness,
I would find meaning in my life.
I was wrong.

Happiness can't be forced.
It's always a by-product.

I thought I could get meaning for my life
by getting it from my significant relationships.

I was wrong.

If I don't take meaning into a relationship,
I will never get any meaning out of it.

I thought God
had the meaning for my life.

I was wrong.

God gives me life,
not meaning.

What I give back to God in my life
is the meaning I seek.

A LEGACY

She was thirty-seven and the mother of three children. She was troubled because she couldn't seem to want to go back to her childhood home and be with her parents when holidays obligated her. There was a sense of aloofness, distance, and coldness with her mother. But she decided to go and visit her parents.

When she got back to her childhood home, she was in the kitchen with her mother, helping to prepare the family dinner. As she was working with her hands, her head bowed, she began a long-awaited conversation with her mother. A conversation she had rehearsed in therapy several times.

"Mom, when I was a little girl, why didn't you hug me more often? Why didn't you tell me that you loved me? Whenever I would go and stay the night at my girlfriend's house, her mother would come in at night and hug her and squeeze her and stroke her head and tell her she loved her. I was so envious of them. Whenever you came in at night before going to bed, I would wish expectantly for you to hug and kiss me good night, but all you would do was lay my clothes out for the following day. It's like you were more concerned about what other people were thinking and saying than you were about me."

Her mother, with tears filling her eyes, looked at her daughter and said, "Oh, my child, didn't you know? Didn't I ever tell you? When I was a little girl, I had to go to school every day wearing dirty, wrinkled clothes. I swore to God, if I should ever have a daughter like you, that would never happen! When I laid your clothes out each night, that was my way of hugging you. That was my way of saying I love you. Didn't you know?"

For nearly thirty years this daughter held on to this resentment before she had this conversation with her mother, and her mother had not been able to say the words every child hungers to hear on a regular basis: "I love you." More than thirty Mother's Days had come and gone with this invisible wedge between them. These two found each other, and Mother's Day would never be the same again. Indeed.

HAZARDS

My memory can be hazardous.
 I find myself recalling
 every raised eyebrow

every embarrassing moment
every slight
every let-down
every put-down.

My memory can be hazardous.
 I get tangled up
 in guilt and shame.
 I get smothered by my success
 and choke on sobs nobody cares.

I need to heal this hazardous memory.
 But this won't come through revenge.
 I must refuse to dwell on how I've been hurt
 and dwell on how I've been helped.

I need to heal this hazardous memory.
 I need to stop hiding behind
 my hurts and grudges,
 the tons of disappointments,
 the list of betrayals.

No matter how hard I try to hide
 God keeps finding me,
 and I hear that familiar whisper,
 "Billy, it's time to come out of hiding.
 It's time to risk again."

REALITY CHECK

I used to be an avid skier, but Parkinson's has taken its toll on my love for the sport. I know that as the Parkinson's progresses, my ability to ski will decrease. Even now, I ski only when "accompanied by an adult." Recently, I flew to Utah to ski with a colleague for a day in Park City. I was concerned this would be my last chance to ski.

The problem with Parkinson's lies in its ability to keep the brain from cooperating with what the body wants to do. It's also on my left side, and when fatigued, my left side shuts down. Knowing this, I went skiing, supervised. When I fall, without help, I can rarely get up on my own.

The first two hours of skiing were glorious! I was being careful, but I was skiing and doing quite well. I couldn't ski fast or ski on advanced slopes, but I was skiing. Then we quit for lunch. I could tell I needed to rest. But not long. I came here to ski, not sit in a warming hut.

I jumped off the ski lift on the far side of the ski area. It would be my moment of truth. I started to ski down a beautiful face of snow, but something was wrong. I couldn't make the turns, and I began to fall. I was able to stand up, but my body wouldn't respond to my brain and again I fell.

My anxiety level started to go off the charts. My confidence was gone, and suddenly this beautiful hill of snow became my arch enemy.

My colleague was at the bottom of the hill, helplessly watching this all play out. I am falling and sliding down the slope, and now I am completely out of control.

Somehow, I was able to stop the slide and I found a way to get up. I had a long way to get to the bottom of the hill. I turned my skis downward, and I barely made ten feet before I fell for the last time. This fall had me slide into a tree that kept me from falling into a deep ravine. I knew then I couldn't go on. That's when a member of the ski patrol came up behind me. His name was Bob, middle fifties, from Canada.

He said, "I've watched you come down this slope for the last half hour. I know you're a good skier. What's wrong?"

"I think I'm in trouble. I have Parkinson's, and it has decided to shut my body down. I don't know if I can get up, and even if I do, I don't think I can negotiate the descent down the mountain. The left side of my body has frozen up, and my balance is marginal."

"Bill, we're going to sled you down to the main lodge. Let me call it in. Do you have any meds?"

"They're in the car. As for the sled, no deal. This may be my last skiing experience, and I refuse to have it end with me in a sled. We have to figure something out. I need your help to get me down, but I'm going down with my skis on, even if it means falling down three slopes."

"Bill, it's too dangerous. I know you're frustrated and angry with yourself, but I have to think of your safety and the safety of others. Now let me call for a sled."

"No!" I said. "There has to be another way!"

Bob looked at me for the longest moment. And then he smiled and said, "All right. We'll try it your way first, but if it doesn't work, we get the sled. Okay?"

"Deal."

He helped me get on my feet, walked me down the rest of the slope, repaired one of my bindings, and then said, "Bill, I have a plan. It's going to take at least an hour to get you down. I'm calling ahead to other ski patrollers, and we are going to team up and guide you down around the mountain on a trail used by our plows. It's an easy grade, and I think you can do it."

I thanked Bob for the effort he was making to get me down, and we began the descent. I had to rest several times because my balance was so compromised. The fatigue was overwhelming. The anxiety and tremoring were in control. The stiffness on my left side was fighting all the skills needed for skiing. But an hour later, with the help of a Canuck, I made it down safely.

"Bill," Bob said, "I know you're a good therapist, and I respect you for the work you have provided to people in their greatest need. But I hope you will get your head out of your ass and realize this disease isn't going away. You need to change some of your expectations. Good luck."

Bob was right. I've got some work to do. I need to make peace with this disease. Now, where am I going to go skiing next December?

A ROOM WITHOUT A VIEW

I have a room
I go to on occasion.
It's dark, foreboding, cold, and damp.
It's called the room of remorse.

This is a room
I go into whenever I get depressed.
I crawl inside this room and I begin
to think of all my mistakes,
all my regrets.

In this room,
I grieve over all the things
I wished I hadn't done
the things I should have done
and didn't do.

This is the room
where I can breathe my mistakes
where I can re-live my shame
where I can ponder my ugliness
where the ghosts can haunt me.

From this room
I yearn to be released
To be free to know that life can begin again
To be free of the prison of the past
To dwell in the room of forgiveness.

A WAITING FATHER

I remember when I was eight years old. The second oldest of four boys. We lived in a rural area of western New York. It was a wonderful place to grow up. We lived on a lake, there were four seasons, we had a boat, and my dad was a well-known fisherman and boat man in the area. We did so much together. I adored my father.

One day, after school, about four o'clock, I asked my father if I could go up the street and play with some friends. He said it would be fine but to remember that dinner was at six o'clock and I had better not be late. He said that while looking directly at me, and I sensed he wasn't kidding. The message was clear. Don't be late!

I lost track of the time. When the sun was setting I realized it was well past the time I was expected to be home. I asked my friend's mother what time it was, and she said it was 6:20. I raced out of the house and ran down the street toward home. As I neared my home, there standing in the middle of the street was my father with his hands on his hips. I knew I was in serious trouble.

I stopped running because I was crying so hard. I had let my father down, and I knew I was going to be punished for not keeping my word. As I neared my father, my crying turned to sobbing. I was so afraid of what the consequences were going to be.

When I reached my father, I sobbed, "Daddy, I didn't mean to be late. I'm sorry. I'm so sorry!"

He knelt down, pulled me into his arms, and held me until I stopped crying. Then he said,

"Son, you have punished yourself more than I would have ever punished you. You're home now, and I'm just glad that you are safe."

He picked me up in his arms and took me home to dinner. No allowance for two weeks!

I didn't know then I would have this hero in my life for only seven more years. My father would be diagnosed with a rare disease that would take five years to kill him. I would eventually become his primary caregiver. While my mother had to work, and when my father was out of remission, I would be the one to bathe him, light his cigarettes, make sure his paperwork for his business was in order, and stay with him for hours to make sure he was safe.

Little did I know I was being trained to become a caregiver to those who were soon to die. Little did I know my father would become my first patient.

AND SO IT GOES

It was late, and the storm was relentless, even for the Pacific Northwest. As I turned in to go to bed, I was thinking of how relieved I felt that I didn't have to be anywhere that night. Just as I crawled into bed, I heard someone pounding on my front door and the person seemed to be calling out my name. I was alone in my Seattle home, and all the lights were out.

I got up, put on my bathrobe, and went to the door. I turned on the porch light and yelled through the front door, "Who is it? Who's out there?"

A moaning, sobbing voice responded as the person continued pounding on the door. "Please, please let me in. I can't live like this any longer! Please!"

I opened the door and in stumbled this elderly woman, soaked from the rain. Her hair was disheveled and dripping from the storm. She was shivering from the cold, wet, sobbing through it all and unable to make any sense of her situation.

I turned on the heat, lit a fire, and started the coffee. I sensed that this was going to be a long night. Then I suggested she go in and shower and get some dry clothes I had selected I thought she could wear.

I said, "Mrs. Truxton, I insist that you do these few things or I won't be able to help you. But if you shower and change, this will give you a few moments to breathe and calm yourself so that we can talk this through. Otherwise, I need to call 911."

Thirty minutes later, she came back into the living room, sat down, and just stared at the floor. There was little improvement of her state of mind. "Why did you come here, Mrs. Truxton, and how did you find me?"

She said, "I heard you give a lecture about your work with the terminally ill. And, you're in the phone book. Dr. Stephenson, I need your help. Ever since my husband died, I haven't been able to function. I can't live like this any longer. You've got to take my case. You've got to!"

I never see clients in my home and rarely see adults without children in a life-threatening crisis, but saying no to someone in distress at midnight didn't seem like a good idea. "Mrs. Truxton, tell me your story."

"Just before my husband died, we had a terrible argument. Before we went to bed, I screamed at him, 'I wish you were dead!' The next morning, I woke up and next to me was my dead husband."

She said, "I am responsible for my husband's death. It's my fault. I have been burdened by this guilt. I was too distraught to go to the funeral. I often never get out of bed. I don't know how to live alone. I cry constantly. I rarely venture out of the house. I've stopped seeing my friends or going to my church because I just keep crying. Even my children have grown weary of me, and they don't want the grandchildren around me. My world has come to an end, and all I want to do is die."

As the hour of counseling came to a close, I decided to extend it to two. Both of us exhausted, we set up a schedule of times we would meet, including the next day. I asked her if she thought she could drive home, and she reassured me that she was very capable. The storm outside and the storm inside seemed to be abating.

"Mrs. Truxton, do you have feelings of wanting to kill yourself?"

"Not anymore, Dr. Stephenson. I feel like I have some hope that I haven't had for a long time."

Just as she was leaving, I asked her, "By the way, Mrs. Truxton, I meant to ask you, how long ago did your husband die?"

She said, "It's been eleven years ago yesterday. And it seems like it was only yesterday."

It would take several months of therapy and medication management to resolve the issues in her life. Grief is a strange animal, and time doesn't heal all wounds. In fact, for Mrs. Truxton, her watch had stopped.

MY RESOURCE

As I begin this new day,
my soul waits for God
to come gently into my life
like the fading of dark and daybreak.

I yearn to awaken
all the resources of my faith
lest I measure my hope
by the mood of the moment
and miss what this new day
has in store for me.

As I begin this new day,
I now open myself to this gentleness,
reminding myself
that God is already within me.

As I accept this gentle strength
I am then able to have the wisdom
to share.

FISHING WITH BREAD

Our cruise ship ported at Mykonos, a small island off the coast of Greece, for an overnight stay. Early the next morning, before sunrise, I went for a walk along the pier. All was quiet, and as the sun began to rise, I could see a man fishing about a quarter of a mile down from the ship. As I came up to him, I was to meet an old man, chain-smoking and fishing with gear that might have been on display in an antique shop.

I introduced myself, and he spoke very little English. But he was willing to stumble through the limits of our separate languages, and we got to know each other. I eventually asked him if I could borrow his fishing pole and fish for a half hour. He smiled and said he'd be honored. He reeled in his line, and there were over a dozen small hooks attached to the line, all empty of bait. I asked, "What do you use for bait?"

"Bread! Of course!"

"How do you keep the bread on the hook once it gets in the water?"

He smiled and said, "I show you." And he went into his old beat-up car and pulled out a piece of very stale, very hard bread. He looked at me and instructed: "You bite into bread and then put on hook! No?"

We both smiled, and we both bit into this very hard loaf of bread. Two old men, one from a wealthy and powerful nation, and the other, toothless and weather-worn from an island I could barely pronounce. Neither one of us could speak the other's language, but it didn't matter.

We took the chewed bread out of our mouths, and together we attached it to the hooks and began to giggle like two kids playing hooky with a fishing pole. We cast the line into the water, continued to chew on this very hard bread, and waited in silence.

I suddenly realized I was on holy ground. Two old men, from very different countries far apart, coming together and discovering we both had the same address. We both realized we belonged to the same family. We were brothers forever after this fishing tale would come to an end.

Whenever I feel like I've forgotten where I live, and I do often when senseless violence is committed . . . Dallas, Orlando, Minneapolis, Baton Rouge, Las Vegas . . . I forget sometimes where I am living. That is when I close my eyes and remember a toothless old man with a cigarette dangling from his mouth, helping me bait a hook. Then I remember my address: The human family. The Mind of God.

FREEDOM FROM FEAR

A crisis counseling organization asked me to be a part of a team made up of nine other therapists from around the United States. We would be trained and then sent on a moment's notice to places that had experienced a traumatic event in the community. We were to equip and train those professionals in that community to better assist their citizens who were suffering from traumatic or complicated grief, the fear of it occurring again, the anger and frustration and powerlessness that often comes from an unwanted tragedy.

One such event occurred in the East. For nearly two weeks I worked with those in the community who were specifically dedicated to the children who had been traumatized. The background to this story is that a man had gone into a community center of this small town and killed five people and then himself.

Children were having night terrors. They were afraid of their parents leaving the house for fear they would not come back. They didn't want to go to school or play outside for fear that something would happen to them. Parents and teachers felt powerless in trying to convince many of the children this would not happen again.

I selected seven children who were particularly traumatized. They had all lost someone close to them in the massacre. In an auditorium, I had the children sit on stage in a circle. The auditorium was filled with teachers, social workers, clergy, other children, friends, and family.

I asked the children if they would describe their feelings about the massacre. They were eager to share the anxiety and fear, but they were consistently told by those around them they had nothing to be afraid of. This would not happen to them. Nevertheless, they all described how they couldn't sleep. They were always anxious about being outside. They described waiting for their father and mother to come home and crying if they were late. They were all in grief, and it seemed as if they could not get past that horrible day when someone came into their community center and started killing.

I asked them, "Do you know who did this?"

"No," said everyone in the circle.

"Have you ever seen him or a picture of this man?"

And everyone said emphatically, "No!"

"How do you feel about this man?"

One boy said, "I wish I could kill him!" And others began to express similar feelings. I could see that as they began to express these emotions they were moving out of fear and into anger. Moving out of a non-cognitive position to a cognitive position.

I said, "I have a picture of the man who did this. Would you let me show it to you?" They all agreed, and I could sense the anxiety of those in the audience. I put the picture in the middle of the circle so that all the children could see the picture together and at the same time. There was complete silence in the group and in the audience.

After a couple of minutes, I asked the children what they were feeling. One boy said, "I want to stomp on his face!"

I said, "Go ahead. No one will stop you." And immediately he jumped up and went to the center of the circle and began stomping on the picture and yelling. Soon others got up and began to stomp on the picture and then others until all the children had the opportunity to vent their anger.

Some of the children were crying, but it was a cry of relief. Others began to pace, and some quietly returned to their seats. Those in the audience were also reacting with crying and wanting to come up and support the children.

After everyone had calmed down, I asked, "Now that you have stomped on his picture, is anyone in the circle feeling afraid?"

"I'm not afraid anymore. I'm just angry!" And the others agreed.

I turned to the audience of caregivers and supporters of these children and said, "Now it's your turn. Children have not yet learned how to be afraid and angry at the same time. That part of their brain has not yet developed. But now their fear is gone. Now it's your responsibility to work with these children to move beyond their anger. They are now dealing with this trauma in the present and not out of what could happen. Affirm, don't judge, their anger. It's a healthy emotion. Your job is to show them now how they will use their anger to get well again. Good luck."

I turned to the children and asked if they had anything else to say. And they rushed toward me and gave me a big collective hug. I still hear from some of those children who are now young adults. They still have recall of that tragic moment. But they also remind me they have learned to take back their lives because of that day on a stage in a school auditorium, with a man they saw only a couple of times, but taught them the power of being free from fear.

ON FALLING

My soul conflicts with my fear of dying.

To reduce that fear,
I will seek to know the Great Adventure,
and to trust.

I will choose to pick my life up again
with a new joy.

I will find the courage to wait in the silence
and trust in the darkness.

When the thread of life breaks
and I fall,
underneath are God's everlasting arms.

A RECURRING NIGHTMARE

M onica was just twenty-seven. She was single. She called herself a born-again Christian. She had no family that came to visit her as I recall. She was dying of cancer. She asked for me.

I would come to her bedside, and we would talk. Well, she did the talking. She talked incessantly. She talked about her childhood and adolescence. She talked about both of her marriages. She talked about her two miscarriages and one abortion. She owned a lot of unresolved grief and a load of guilt that clashed with her beliefs.

But throughout all her conversations she kept reminding me, or herself, how she had come to know Jesus and the conversional moment when she accepted Christ into her life. It was just after she had been diagnosed with fourth stage lymphocytic leukemia.

She shared with me the extensive and painful treatment she had undergone. She said, "My fellow church members had been so supportive in the beginning, but now that I have been diagnosed as terminal, they seemed less so." She said, "They don't know what to say, so they stay away."

She was not the same Monica they had known. She now had no hair, was emaciated and in constant need of transfusions. There would be no remission for her. She said when people looked at her she could see their fear. Her visitor's registration book was nearly empty.

She seemed dismayed, unsure, anxious. I continued to counsel her on her current state, and I remained committed to assisting her in staying in the moment, staying in the present, knowing her death was imminent.

She continued each session with her confidence in Jesus, believing he would save her so she could go on missionary trips around the world. She said, "I am determined that if I get out of the hospital, I will dedicate the rest of my life to service for others."

She continued to be in terrible pain, but she refused all pain medications. The pain medications could manage the pain without rendering her unconscious, but she felt the need to stay alert and wait for one more round of chemotherapy that would save her life. But there would not be one more round.

Late one weekend afternoon, when many of the patients in the hospice were out visiting family or going for a walk, Monica used that time to talk to the staff about her faith and how she was ready, as she said, "to go be with Jesus." Her ability to thrive was declining rapidly, and early that same evening, she collapsed.

She was put in her bed, and the hospice team did everything they could to make her comfortable. She was close to death, but she asked I come to her bedside as soon as possible. When I arrived, she began to cry. It was a frightened cry, like a small child who was lost with no one to help her.

"Dr. Stephenson, is it time for me to die? I'm not ready yet. I'm not ready yet. I don't want to die. I don't want to die! Please. Hold me. I'm so scared!"

I reached down and took her in my arms and held her, but she continued to cry, and her distress now became known by everyone around us. It was as if no one could understand what needed to be done. Monica suddenly hemorrhaged. She began to expel blood from her mouth, nose, and rectum.

I continued to hold her as she kept pleading, "I don't want to die! I don't want—" Then, she lost consciousness, and died soon after.

I don't remember much of what transpired after that. Nurses said I was covered in blood. They tried to speak to me, but they could tell I was not able to hear them. They said I was unable to speak or respond to any voice for nearly three days. Weeks went by, and I had night terrors that disrupted my household. I wasn't fit to see clients, I was scaring my own children, I lost weight.

Therapy, especially group therapy, helped me get past what I judged to be my biggest failure. I would have other "failures" that would challenge my commitment to this work I had chosen for myself, but Monica's death reminded me of ghosts that would haunt me and wake me up in a cold sweat on occasion.

HOPE DISGUISED

I have two grandsons: Liam, who is two, and Noah, who is four. They're brothers, and they do everything together. I decided to take them fishing. Taking a two-year-old fishing is an event that only another grandfather can appreciate. Noah, well, he was focused on getting a big fish. Liam, he was focused on getting in the water!

I had given each of them their own fishing pole, and they could hardly wait to test it out on a lake I had never fished. I began to get Liam's pole ready, but then he saw the playground nearby and off he went. Noah, on the other hand, had wanted to fish with Popi and seemed to be relieved that Liam had decided to go play.

Unfortunately, my Parkinson's began to raise its ugly head. The tremors became significant, and the anxiety that goes with them became obvious. As I began to try and bait Noah's hook, the tremors began to win, and no matter how hard I tried, I couldn't get the bait on his hook. Tears came to my eyes as I wanted so much to have this precious time fishing with this child I loved so much.

It was as if Noah was reading my mind. This four-year-old child, with the wisdom of one so much older, turned to me and said, "Popi, please. Take my hand, and together we will make your shaking stop. Just take my hand."

I looked at this child for the longest moment, and I reached out and gave him my hand. He held it close to his chest and said, "Popi, you will be okay." And miraculously, I was.

Within moments, my tremoring and other Parkinson symptoms ebbed, and together we were able to bait his hook.

Hope was found in this child who became my guardian angel for just a few moments. I am learning that hope often comes that way. It's disguised, unrecognizable sometimes, but always there, found through my willingness to be open to the moment.

A postscript. Noah would catch the biggest bass I have ever seen caught! No one believed that a four-year-old could catch such a trophy fish. Liam? He wanted to hold my hand and go for a walk. Indeed.

HOW FAR

When I look at some of my relationships,
I'm as far as East is to West!
Endless.

I seem to be remedial
in forgiveness and caring,
but a scholar at what I believe.
Incongruent.

I have mastered communicating
by texting, emailing, and Facebook.
But I'm still struggling with
communication across the dinner table.
Listen.

And I struggle with the "Outsiders."
Surely the ones who don't love God
are outside of the beloved community.
Surely.

But are those I perceive as outsiders,
on the outside?
Really?

Perhaps I will get closer to my soul
if I expand my understanding of community
and include those that God loves as well.
Finally.

GIVE ME TOMORROW

Veterans Day is a day set aside to remember the many men and women who have served our country to preserve our freedoms and give us hope that there will be a tomorrow. These two reports represent that hope we all share and cherish.

During the Korean War, a news correspondent had gone over to Korea, right to the borderline, where eighteen thousand American Marines were about to be pitted in battle against a hundred thousand Communist troops. It was New Year's Day. It was bitterly cold. The Marines, each of them, knew his odds of survival.

At midnight, supper was served: cold beans, to be eaten beside their tanks. One big fellow, his clothes frozen and mud encrusted in his beard, stood by his tank eating his meal with his trench knife.

The correspondent, feeling quite philosophical, approached him and said, "Young man, if I were God and I could give anything you wanted in the whole world, what would you want?"

Knowing the odds of survival that night, the young soldier didn't hesitate. He said, "I'd want you to give me tomorrow." His plea for hope.

And then beyond death—the Holocaust. Six million Jews killed. What hopeful word? When our troops liberated one of the death camps, this story of hope was reported by one of the survivors.

He recounted watching an elderly Jew, standing with his grandson by a trench, both about to be shot to death. The survivor said to the American soldier, "Just before their row of humanity was to be added to the others already lying dead in the trench, the old man raised his hand and pointed up."

In each of these stories, both men are facing death and both chose to face it with the hope that there will be another day. Even after death. Another day. A different kind of tomorrow. A different kind of hope.

PANIC AND A PEACEFUL HEART

// I was so ashamed, I could just die." That is what he said, and then he did. They don't know whether he died because he was ashamed for lying or because he was caught in a lie. But the last thing he said was, "I'm so ashamed, I could die." And he did. Then his wife, hours later, also died.

This story is not some television reality show episode. It's a story found in the Bible in the Book of Acts. Two people who went into a panic collapsed and died when faced with the painful truth. As physicians well know, the body has a way of acting out what the mind believes.

Dr. George Engel, in an article published in the *Annals of Internal Medicine*, entitled, "Sudden and Rapid Death during Psychological Stress," reports the results of a study of persons who died after receiving some distressing news.

The greatest single category of sudden death from stress or emotional shock were those who had been suddenly confronted with some grave personal danger. The second largest category of sudden death due to stress were those who had heard of the death or serious injury of a loved one. The third greatest category of those who died of sudden death due to emotional shock, Dr. Engel found, were those who suffered from some severe humiliation and recognition that their personal status had been wounded. Interestingly enough, more men than women died in that category of severe humiliation and battered egos.

I had a client who was discouraged and depressed and saw himself as a failure. Doctors said there was nothing physically wrong with him, but in spite of what the doctors said, he lost his will to live, his heart got the message, and it obeyed.

Dr. Engel's study affirms that our minds are miraculous, and they have a great deal of power over the behavior of our bodies. Which begs the question: Is panic contagious? Can we catch it from each other?

The *Los Angeles Times* reported an event that happened at a high school football game in nearby Monterey Park. Four spectators, during a game, came and reported they were nauseous and vomiting and felt faint. A quick conclusion was made that there was food poisoning from an orange drink at the snack bar because of some copper wiring. Because the loudspeakers weren't working, they instructed the cheerleaders to go in front of the bleachers and tell the crowd not to drink the orange drink because food poisoning was suspected.

Within minutes, nearly two hundred people reported being nauseous and began to vomit and faint. By ambulances and private cars, they were all rushed to emergency rooms at nearby hospitals.

But it was a false alarm. While the doctors all found them suffering from symptoms of food poisoning, when they were analyzed, none of the food or drink in that snack bar was contaminated. When the people were told that, their symptoms left them as quickly as they had come.

Behavior is contagious. What we put into our minds affects our bodies, and if I may use computerese: "Garbage in, garbage out. What we put into our minds matters a great deal.

The late Dr. Norman Cousins, in his book *The Healing Heart*, tells of an experience he had on a golf course. He noticed an ambulance and paramedics working on a man lying on a stretcher. Because Cousins himself was a survivor of a massive heart attack, he rushed over and noticed that the paramedics were doing what they were trained to do. Everyone was watching the gauges and monitors they had hooked up to the man. But no one was looking at the man.

Cousins looked at the man's face and saw his panic and then saw that the cardiac monitor indicated that his heartbeat was so rapid that he was about to go into shock, and so he went over and put his hand on the man and said, "You've got a fine heart."

The man said, "How do you know?"

"I can see it on the cardiograph. And, furthermore, you're about to be taken to one of the finest hospitals in the country and you're going to be just fine."

The man's panic began to subside because something else was going into his mind, and he began to look around and became interested and involved in what was happening. Dr. Cousins went on to say to him, "It's a hot day, and you're de-hydrated, and that effects the electrical shocks in your heart, and you're going to be all right." And he was.

What we put into our minds has a great deal to do with whether panic will dwell in our hearts. Garbage in, garbage out.

Francis MacNutt, a pioneer in the limitless possibilities of the human spirit, tells a story his mother told about him when he was a little boy. He was being punished by his mother, and she said, "Francis, you have to go and stand in that corner." In recalling that incident, his mother said that Francis replied to her, "Mother, I refuse to regard this as a corner!" You can't worry about a boy like that.

But that's what we need to tell ourselves when we are in a crisis. I remind my clients that they have options. They get to select their emotions and their reactions to stressful events. They may not be able to change those circumstances, but they can choose their attitude toward those circumstances and that may make all the difference. It may even save their lives.

THE ART OF TRAPEZING

To laugh is to risk appearing a fool
  To weep is to risk appearing sentimental
   To reach out is to risk involvement
     To expose feelings is to risk exposing one's true self
      To place our ideas before others is to risk rejection

To love is to risk being loved
  To live is to risk dying
   To hope is to risk despair
     To try is to risk failure

The greatest tragedy is to not risk at all.
  Change, recovery, reconciliation and harmony
     Only comes to those who are willing---

                    --- To risk

THE ART OF WAITING

L ife is filled with waiting, and sometimes it's as if the world is one large waiting room. Some people feel like that character in William Saroyan's play, *The Time of Your Life*, who says, "The more you wait, the less there is to wait for." A lot of people grow tired of waiting. They get impatient, and they quit. Waiting is such an important part of our lives. It is crucial to learn how to wait creatively, expectantly, and hopefully.

I was asked to counsel a family whose newborn son was born with his brain outside of his skull. He lived for seventeen days. His entire family—mother, father, grandparents, aunts, uncles, cousins—all surrounded this baby with love. But to care for this newborn, and each other, they had to learn to wait lovingly, effectively, creatively, unselfishly. Otherwise, in time, the tension and anxiety would become so great that waiting for the baby to die could begin to destroy one another. There is a kind of waiting that is destructive.

A married couple came for counseling. They were so close on many things. However, she had a deeply religious experience that changed her life. She wanted her husband to share it with her. But her waiting for him to share in this religious lifestyle was done arrogantly and smugly. Her religious experience would eventually drive them apart even with the counseling. She knew how to believe, but she didn't know how to wait. She wouldn't learn how to wait creatively and lovingly.

One young woman was twenty-one years old. She went through a passage of rebellion in which she did some things that were unthinkable by most people. Her parents judged she was permanently lost to the street. They told her they could not tolerate her behavior any longer. Telling her this broke their relationship. This young lady, with professional care, was able to get through that passage, but not with them, without them. Despite attempts to bring them together, no words were exchanged. The parents didn't know how to wait, creatively, lovingly.

It's the quality of waiting that makes the difference whether or not a relationship will survive. That quality comes when we are able to alter our expectations about the future because that is what brings power into the present.

THE ORIGINAL SIN

In a very intimate workshop I was leading, a middle-aged man made this confession:

"Nothing I ever did won my parents' approval. As I look back on it now, if I got B's and C's, they'd say I should have gotten all A's and B's. When I achieved that one year, they had new goals for me: my posture was bad; my table manners were atrocious; I should be more polite; keep my room neater; do more around the house."

He said, "I got so little approval. They just kept setting the standards higher and higher, and I never made it. I probably never will make it because I have some irrational, perfectionistic standard imprinted on my brain. I know in my head that my parents were wonderful people. I hate criticizing them, yet I resent their making me earn their approval by being perfect.

"After I got out of school and succeeded pretty well in my first job, my father offered some warm approval. I heard him, but it didn't register. The feeling was, 'It's too late, Dad. I needed that a long time ago. Your acceptance is about twenty years too late.' He often expressed pride in my achievements after that, but I could never accept it. It didn't matter whether he approved of me now or not. I had shut him out long before.

"But now I feel guilty for having transmitted this perfectionistic approach on to my children!"

This may be another definition of Original Sin.

THE SECRET TO THE JOURNEY

In Thornton Wilder's play, *Our Town,* there is one scene that helps me find my center. This little girl has just moved to a small town. She is not feeling well, and she is lonely. An older friend, knowing how she must be feeling, sends her a letter. It isn't what he writes in the letter but how he addresses the envelope that communicates the most. On the envelope, he writes:

Jane Crofut
Crofut Farms
Grover's Corners, New Hampshire

Not with a zip code that would get it there, but with a message that would tell her something. Under Grover's Corners, New Hampshire, he added:

The United States of America
The Continent of North America
The Western Hemisphere
The Earth
The Solar System
The Universe

And then, in big letters he wrote:

THE MIND OF GOD

When pressures begin to build up and you find yourself frantically trying to get other people to tell you that you are okay...or, if you find yourself trying to please others to feel of value, then pause, and take the time to center. Find your address:

> In God, I live and move and have my being.
> In God, I live and move.
> In God, I live.
> In God.
>> This is the secret to the journey.

GIFT TO SELF

There are days
I need to stop,
check my address,
to know who I am,
and whose I am.

To find again the secret to the journey.

When I feel frayed, frazzled and frightened,
When I am hurting, hassled and hungry,
I must remember that what I search for,
is a gift I already have within me,
waiting to be re-discovered.

CHAPTER FOUR

THE SEASON OF BEGINNINGS AND BEGINNINGS AGAIN

PREPARING FOR CHRISTMAS

God doesn't ask us
to believe in the future.
God calls us
to believe the future in.
Without vision
people perish.

God doesn't ask us
to believe in love.
God asks us to believe love in,
by what we do and say
in our relationships
and daily priorities.

As I prepare for Christmas,
I am reminded
that I make my own decisions.
"What am I doing?"
"How am I preparing?"
"How am I relating?"

This Christmas,
will I languish in the darkness
or light a candle?

THE DEVIL IN CHRISTMAS-A LEGEND

Once upon a time, so the story goes, the devil became deeply disturbed. Now those of you who know the literature and legends about the devil know that he's a pretty cunning character and he does not get disturbed very easily.

But he was on this occasion because he was alarmed at the prospect of the whole world becoming fascinated with the story of Christmas. That is, becoming so charmed with the beauty of the story, so enchanted by the angelic music that tugs on one's heart, so warmed by the spirit of peace and goodwill, that the people would begin to actually believe that God would sneak into this world disguised as a baby, and if they did they'd never be the same again.

The devil knew that something drastic had to be done so the people could somehow get through Christmas without Christmas getting through to them. The devil knew that some device had to be developed so that people could move through Christmas without ever allowing Christmas to move them. Some strategy that would be so subtle people would not even know it was happening to them.

Could it be done? Lo and behold, the devil devised a diabolical scheme that has outdone everything else his evil mind had ever conjured up. In order to keep people from experiencing Christmas, the devil devised what is now popularly called the Christmas rush!

People are so caught up with the outward expressions of the day, they miss its simplicity. So absorbed in the pressures and promotions, so guilty about the demands and obligations: "Did you remember to send Uncle Harry a card? And what about the Smiths? Should we keep them on the list this year? And do you think the children are going to appreciate what we took out three installments to buy them?"

So caught up in the fussing and the fuming we miss the meaning that really matters: the profound word about what is really eternal. The message of Christmas gets lost in our anxious agenda of all that we've just got to get done before the stores close! The frantic feeling that we go through the Christmas season with far too much to do and far too little time to do it.

Of course, this is just a legend, and this legend should not be taken seriously. Unless, of course, that's also a part of the devil's strategy.

Author's note: After extensive research, I could not find the source for this fable.

AN UNCOMMON PSALM
FOR CHRISTMAS

I need to remember that for many
Christmas is a lonely time.

I want to be sensitive
to this loneliness of others
and reach out as I can.

But,
I know that I am lonely as well.

I must remember that loneliness is not to be feared.
There is a sense of solitude
that gives me the strength to know
the unbreakable oneness I have
in silence with God.

CHRISTMAS FOR BEGINNERS

A colleague was asked to work with a sixth grade Sunday School class during the Christmas season. She gave them as their assignment for the next four Sundays the task of translating the Christmas story into twenty-first-century symbols that would be relevant to their culture. This is their translation.

The President and Congress sent out a request to all the citizens of the United States to register themselves for a tax count. This was the first enrollment since Obama became president. Everyone went to his own city to enter his name on the tax list.

A man named Joseph went up from Atlanta to Detroit, the city of cars, with his wife, Mary. She was to have a baby and she gave birth to her first son.

Now for those children, unfamiliar with a stable and a manger, what would be a current symbol of hopelessness?

And Mary gave birth to her first son in the back of a gas station in a large shopping center because all the motels were full up and they could not find a place to stay. She dressed her son in a jumpsuit and laid him in a shopping cart padded with newspapers.

The next task was to translate the cast of characters, the shepherds, and angels.

And in that day there were policemen keeping watch over the city. Suddenly, the extraterrestrials (ETs) appeared and the sky was lighted up. The policemen were filled with fear, and the extraterrestrials said, "Be not afraid. For look! We have brought you happiness. For to you today is born in Detroit a baby who is named Jesus! And this will be a signal for you to find the child. You will find the baby wearing a jumpsuit and lying in a shopping cart padded with newspapers."

And suddenly there was a mob of extraterrestrials singing and saying, "Glory to God in the highest and peace on earth and peace to those with whom God is well pleased."

Who is to say that these sixth graders, in translating these first-century symbols into their twenty-first-century experience, have not been just as faithful as the best of biblical scholars? In translating shepherds into policemen, swaddling clothes into a jumpsuit, a manger and stable into a broken-down shopping cart behind an old gas station, these children have once again done what we adults have such a hard time doing—of maintaining the surprise of the birth of Christ in the midst of the mundane, the commonplace, the everyday stuff of our lives. My point being, you just never know where Christmas is going to happen.

This news item from the Portsmouth News may underscore my point.

> *Ernest Digweed, a Portsmouth schoolteacher, who turned recluse and died at the age of 81, left his fortune of #44,000 to Jesus Christ, according to a Will. The only conditions are that Jesus must arrive within 80 years and be recognized as the Messiah by the public trustee, a state official, or the money will go to the crown.*

> *A spokesman for the public trustee said, "Clearly, Mr. Digweed was a man of religious conviction and was expecting a second coming."*

> *Mr. Digweed lived in squalor under a homemade tent in the front room of his house. He spoke to no one and ignored all knocks at his door.*

Whether it's the squalor of a living room or in a shopping cart behind an old gas station or the scandal within our lives or the shame or disappointment or failure in our relationships . . . you never know where Christmas is going to happen. Christmas can happen anywhere in the midst of our messy lives where we are most disappointed or where our need is deepest.

A CHRISTMAS HOPE

Strangely,
I walk through the days of my years,
unseeing,
unhearing,
inattentive,
afraid.

Though
the glorious fight for life
is all about me,
and I do not even know
the limit of possibilities.

Yet,
I wrap myself up
in the petty and the trivial,
and sometimes
the mean and the sordid,
believing this is all that is real.

As I journey toward Christmas,
I labor to know
how vain are all my hopes,

how empty are all my prayers,
until,
I myself am ready
to believe in them.

CHRISTMAS CALM

It is the eve of Christmas!
Let not the very nearness of your presence
Hide from me in the silence of the night.

O soul,
Be calm so that I can
Hear God breathing close to me,
Nearer to me than my hands and feet.

Silent night, holy night.
Now, all is calm.

THE GIFT OF STAYING

// **Y**ou are before this court to determine whether you are capable of parenting your child. The state has issued a request to take custody of your child because of your physical handicap. How do you plead?" asked the judge.

This is where Jacqueline's story begins. Yet the beginning and end of her story are tightly connected.

The scene in the court room took place thirty-one years ago. Jacqueline appeared in court with her five-month old son. The context of the State's complaint was that Jacqueline was born without any arms or legs. They could find no justification for someone that handicapped being the primary parent of a child. She was confined to a motorized wheel chair she could maneuver with her breath. Otherwise, she needed total care just like her baby.

However, no one in that courtroom knew of her determination and character. She was there to fight for her right and responsibility to raise her son, Steven. Her lawyer presented several character witnesses, all advocating on Jacqueline's behalf.

Then it was Jacqueline's turn to speak or testify to her ability to retain custody of her child. Jacqueline requested permission to demonstrate her ability instead of speaking about it. With her primary care-giver, the three of them proceeded to the center of the courtroom where a changing table was placed for all the powers to see.

Jacqueline then proceeded to undress and redress her infant son by using only her lips and tongue! She did all this in record time, talking to Steven throughout the demonstration. She kissed him and then turned to the judge and said, "I had not planned on getting pregnant, your honor, but I beg of you not to turn this unplanned birth into a tragedy for me and my son. I am a good person and I am determined, with the help of my care-givers, to be an exemplary parent to Steven. Your honor, please don't take Steven from me. Please don't take Steven from his mother."

The judge sat in silence for a significant amount of time, just looking at Jacqueline. Finally, he said, "Never in my courtroom have I witnessed a more courageous act of love and commitment. Ms. Smith, I am so sorry that you were asked to defend the competency of your parental rights. I admonish the State Department of Welfare for ever bringing this to my court. I award you complete custody of your child and can only hope that the two of you will find your future to be a hopeful one. Case dismissed."

It was her son who would tell of their beginning of a life together. He said, "Our life together was not easy. I grew up fast and I was often my mom's primary care-giver. When I wanted to go out and play or participate in a group like the Boy Scouts, or a school activity, instead I was home taking care of my mom. There were times when I resented that obligation. But, today, I now appreciate the devotion we both had to make our relationship work."

He said, "She wants me to go home and take care of my wife and son. But, I'm staying here beside her until the end. She is the one who taught me that. Stay. Hang in there. Don't give up. I can only hope my son will learn that from me."

He was a man of his word. He stayed by his mother's side in the hospice day after day, night after night until she died. He was not going to allow this woman of character, integrity and selfless love die alone. She died on Christmas Eve. It was a good death. Now, all is calm.

CHRISTMAS FOR THE DISILLUSIONED

Let this also be a Christmas
for those who can no longer see You,
for those who cannot hear the newborn cry,
for those who can no longer follow the star.

May Your presence
be placed in their hearts . . .

May Your love
fill their emptiness

May Your light
reach into their darkness . . .

May Your compassion
help them to know what they cannot feel.

May they remember this Christmas
they are never alone because
You see them,
even in their blindness.
You can hear their fearful cry.

May they look for the star . . .
Not in the sky,
but within their own hearts,
and once again find their way to Bethlehem.

A CHRISTMAS EVE PSALM

If
shepherds could be amazed,
kings could be confronted,
wise men could travel from afar,
Then,
I need to remember
there are many ways to the manger,
and there are many longings to love and be loved,
yearning for peace and hope.
Tonight,
I will remember that God has a secret
Stairway
Into
Every
Heart.

Perhaps even,

mine.

CPSIA information can be obtained
at www.ICGtesting.com
Printed in the USA
FSHW04n1720060418
46630FS